BE HAPPY

How To Be Happy At Work and Be A Happier You

PATRICIA DORCH

ALSO BY PATRICIA DORCH

Available

www.amazon.com   www.barnesandnoble.com

Be Happy
How to Be Happy At Work and
Be A Happier You
Visit: howtobehappyatworkbook.com

What Are Soft Skills?
How to Master Essential Skills to Achieve
Workplace Success
Visit: www.whataresoftskills.net

Job Search
College Graduates New Career Advice, Ideas
and Strategies to Get Hired
Visit: www.jobsearchcollegegraduatesbook.com

Professionalism
New Rules for Workplace Career Success
Visit: www.whatisprofessionalism.com

Military to Civilian Transition
Job Search Strategies and Tips to Get Hired
in the Civilian Job Market
Visit: www.militarytociviliantransition.net

Six Figure Career Coaching Advice
The Ultimate Guide to Achieving Success

Job Search
New Get Hired Ideas, Tips and Strategies
for 40 Plus

BE HAPPY

How To Be Happy At Work and Be A Happier You

PATRICIA DORCH

Limit of Liability/Disclaimer of Warranty. The author and publisher have used their best efforts in preparing this book. This publication contains the opinions, ideas and recommendations of its author and publisher. Neither author nor publisher shall be liable for any loss of profit, or risk, personal, including but not limited to special, incidental, consequential, professional or any other commercial or other damages which is incurred as a consequence, directly or indirectly, of the use and application of any of the contents of this book. The accuracy and completeness of the information provided herein and the opinions of stated herein are not guaranteed or warranted to produce any particular results. The advice and strategies contained herein may not be suitable for every individual, organization or situation.

Dorch, Patricia

Be Happy: How to Be Happy At Work and Be A Happier You/Patricia Dorch

Website: www.howtobehappyatworkbook.com
Email: Patricia@howtobehappyatworkbook.com

Website: www.whataresoftskills.net
Email: Patricia@whataresoftskills.net

Website: www.whatisprofessionalism.com
Email: Patricia@whatisprofessionalism.com

Website: www.jobsearchcollegegraduatesbook.com
Email: Patricia@jobsearchcollegegraduatesbook.com

Website: www.militarytociviliantransition.net
Email: Patricia@militarytociviliantransition.net

Printed in the United States of America

ISBN – 13: 978-0-9816854-1-0
ISBN – 10: 0-9816854-1-2

ACKNOWLEDGEMENT

I want to extend my personal and sincere thanks to Robert Moment and all who have dedicated their time, expertise and advice for Be Happy. Your knowledge and support have contributed to my success.

CONTENTS

Choose To Be Happy at Work Starting Today!

Introduction

ARE YOU UNHAPPY AT WORK? Do you want to beat the Monday morning job blues? Do you want to know how successful people achieve happiness at work? If you answered yes to one or more of these questions Be Happy shows you how to transform your career, boost your performance and visibility to be a happier you at work. In today's competitive workplace it takes more than showing up for work, being a good employee and working long hours to make a name for you.

Be Happy: How To Be Happy At Work and Be A Happier You will empower you with secret tips, tools and proven strategies to maximize your unique and valuable skills to be successful and happy at work.

Are You Ready to Be Happy?

In **Part One** – you will learn the *"The Keys to Successful Work Relationships."*

Effective relationships are essential and the foundation to achieve work goals. Your relationships directly impact your well being, job satisfaction and happiness. You will discover:

- How to avoid seven deadly sins of happiness at work.

- Ten new strategies to build a strong relationship with your boss and a roadmap to accomplish work goals for career advancement.

- How to navigate office politics to get things done and avoid being stuck in a dead in job.

- Powerful success tools to build trusting relationships – a critical component to accomplish daily goals, increase productivity and performance.

Do You Need A Plan to Get Ahead?

In **Part Two** you will use a – proven master plan – *"How to Get Ahead and Succeed at Work"* and be a happier you. You will learn:

- Sixteen reasons why a sponsor - a senior level executive has the power and position to fast track your career.

- Twenty one steps to build your personal brand to improve your career options.

- How to determine if your work performance qualifies you for a salary increase before you ask for one.

- Twenty proven strategies to market your "career capital" and increase your income with faster results.

- How smart calculated risk empowers you to increase your performance and success.

Are You Accountable for Your Happiness?

Part Three provides *"Personal and Professional Accountability"* tools you need for career and professional development. You will discover:

- Twenty one happiness rules to be accountable for your happiness at work.

- How introverts can maximize their strengths and minimize weaknesses to excel in a collaborative workplace.

- Good public speaking skills have a profound impact on your career and income.

- How a professional association membership can benefit your career.

Be A Happier You At Work

Inside *Be Happy: How To Be Happy At Work and Be A Happier You* – is a roadmap of proven tips, tools, strategies and techniques you can use starting today. *Be Happy* provides innovative happiness exercises to get you involved to develop your skills, boost productivity and performance. Whether you are starting a new career, or experienced employee *Be Happy* allows you to take control of your happiness at work today.

Are You Ready To Be Happy?

"You have the power to be happy at work"

-Patricia Dorch

BE HAPPY AT WORK

Build strong and internal and external relationships to expand your network.

Enthusiasm is the energy which brings about successful results.

Happiness comes from within.

A happy you at work begin with personal accountability.

Plan for career success.

Personal branding is a career distinction which differentiates you from others.

You are accountable for your happiness at work.

Ask for career advice from sponsors, mentors, managers and career coaches.

Trust is the foundation for meaningful relationships for career growth.

Write your career vision, mission and goals and take action.

Opportunities do not necessarily come to you – you have to make it happen.

Risk empowers you to expand your thinking and set new boundaries.

Knowledge and wisdom are essential keys to success.

Patricia Dorch © Copyright 2016 All Rights Reserved

PART ONE

Keys to Successful
Work Relationships

Chapter 1

Ten Keys to Successful Work Relationships

Do you work well with others? No matter what your generation, education, title or experience the ability to work well with others is essential to your career. Successful work relationships or "people skills" is the foundation for you to accomplish work goals, problem solve, get salary increases, promotions and be successful. These factors contribute to your well being and job happiness.

How you manage work relationships affects your productivity, accomplishments and success. There are ten keys you can use to work well with others starting today.

Key 1: Be a Good Listener. Are you a good listener? To be a good listener you should listen before you speak. Confirm your understanding of the message before you jump to conclusions.

You can do this by repeating back the message to the speaker.

Key 2: Be a Problem Solver – Solution Driven: Can you solve problems? At meetings present ideas to solve problems instead of complaining about them. A solution driven strategy will position you to gain the respect of your manager and peers.

Key 3: Deadlines and Commitments. Do you keep your commitments? Always keep commitments - when you fail to meet obligations your action affects the work of other departments.

If you cannot meet a deadline or commitment let the people know who it will be affected and when they can expect the commitment to be completed. The only excuse which might be acceptable is a family emergency. If you are sick with a cold, forgot to meet the commitment date – these excuses are no longer acceptable in the workplace. It's essential you plan your work and do not wait until the last minute to complete assignments – bottom line your work is expected to be done on time.

Key 4: Motivation. Find out what motivates employees you interact with and spend time in one-on-one informal meetings to find out more about them. Casual conversations about work and pleasure will identify what motivates them – use their motivation to build your relationship.

Key 5: Never Blind Side/Ambush. Have you ever blindsided someone? Never blindside or ambush your manager, co-workers or other staff members. Discuss concerns or problems with them but not in front of others.

Key 6: Don't Play the Blame Game. Do you point your finger at others? Blaming others for your failures will prevent you from building relationships with your co-workers. Build work alliances to support you – not set you up for failure.

Key 7: Share Credit and Contributions. Success is not achieved alone. Take time to thank, acknowledge and reward specific people for their ideas and contributions who help you succeed.

Key 8: Speak Up at Meetings. Do you speak up at meetings? Meetings are a great place to make a contribution and interact with peers and management. Prior to planned meetings take time to think about ideas which may be relevant to meeting topics. Everything you say or do not say will be noted by management.

Key 9: Verbal and Non-Verbal Communication. Do not disrespect, talk down to or use sarcasm to others. It's never acceptable to yell, call names or use inappropriate body language in your communication.

Key 10: Volunteer. Did you know volunteering allows you be visible? Volunteer to take on a project or work on one with your peers improves relationships, increases your skills and makes you more visible. Employees who are visible have the best opportunities for advancement.

Effective work relationships are the foundations for success, satisfaction and happiness. If you implement the keys to successful work relationships you will work well with others and develop strong relationships. Positive relationships will allow you to accomplish work goals and be happy.

Be Happy At Work Essentials

1. Successful work relationships are the foundation for you to accomplish work goals.

2. Positive work relationships affect your productivity, accomplishments and success.

3. Always listen before you speak.

4. Meetings are a great place to make a contribution and interact with peers and management.

5. Find out what motivates your peers and use their motivation to build your relationship.

6. Never blindside or ambush your manager or co-workers.

7. Don't play the blame game. Blaming others will not help you build relationships.

8. Success is not achieved alone – share credit and contributions.

9. Employees who are visible have the best opportunities for advancement.

10. Positive relationships will allow you to accomplish work goals and be happy.

Chapter 2

Trust

How to Cultivate Work Relationships and Build Trust

Are you trustworthy? Can you build and maintain trust in work relationships? A certain level of trust is needed to have a peaceful atmosphere, meet daily work goals to increase productivity. If you do not have trust – you have no relationship.

Does your manager, colleagues, subordinates and superiors see you as trustworthy? Trust builds loyalty, respect and a supportive work environment. Distrust increases a type of "be on guard" behavior and negative work environment which diminishes the team spirit and productivity. Use these tools to build healthy trusting relationships.

Success Tools to Build Trust
in the Workplace

Admit Mistakes. A good relationship does not come without the ability to apologize to correct a mistake. Do not cover up a mistake for fear others will look at you differently – in fact people who admit mistakes are seen as having integrity and trustworthy.

Attitude. We all have personal agendas – however do not hurt others because your focus is entirely on yourself. Increase trust by promoting we not me. Nurture your relationships with a positive attitude and open communication. Be open to constructive critique although it may not be what your want to hear.

Be Accessible. Be accessible to others who look to you for support and information. Do not hide behind a closed door or cubicle – have an open door policy which encourages sharing information and builds trust.

Be Consistent. Be consistent in your behavior and words. Show up to work everyday on time and stay the required work hours. Does your work exceed your employer's expectations? Do more than is expected to fulfill your employment promises.

Be Honest. The most important step in building trust is to be honest. Tell the truth and avoid small lies which become bigger lies. Be honest in all your dealings with others.

Dependable. Be accountable for your actions and responsive to the needs of others. Be organized so others will feel confident knowing they can depend on you to follow through on your promises.

Follow through. When you promise a co-worker you will get back to them about a topic or assignment – follow through in a timely manner. There is nothing more important than your word. Keeping your word on small things demonstrates your dependability and reliability. Follow through builds trust and credibility you will do what you say.

Get to know your co-workers. A genuine friendly and positive attitude will help you get to know your co-workers and build trust. Take time to uncover their professional and personal goals. Getting to know them, their goals and priorities, both in and outside of work will create an atmosphere of trust. Knowing what's going on with them outside of work may be beneficial in understanding their job performance and your relationship with them.

Good judgment. Use good judgment and know whether to share information or not share at all. Think before you speak and reserve your comments about unsolicited judgment about others. Apologies are easier said than accepted or forgotten. Stay clear of conversations which are "just between us" these conversations do not benefit your work environment or build trust.

Gossip. Gossip in the workplace takes away from productivity and increases unnecessary drama. Your involvement in workplace gossip will deem you as a negative person, lower your standards and be seen as untrustworthy.

Increase trust in non-verbal communication. It's estimated more than half our communication is non-verbal. Build trust by maintaining direct eye contact when you speak to co-workers. Exhibit open body language by opening your arms instead of folding them across your chest, remove hands from your pockets or from behind you. When you are seated uncrossed legs with your feet flat on the floor communicates open body language.

Integrity. You should be honest in your dealings with co-workers. Everyone needs to be treated fairly and appropriately for their unique situation. Integrity – doing the right thing when faced with a right or wrong decision.

Leadership. Trusted leaders are essential in the workplace and set the example by being accountable and responsible for their actions. When others have ideas to share a leader should be trusted they will have an open mind.

Share Information. There is power in information. Sharing important information is one of the best ways to build trust. Sharing information communicates a sense of unity to build internal relationships and shared goals.

Building trust is a process which takes time and effort from all parties. Trust can take a long time to build and maintain, but can be destroyed by a single action or miscommunication. Trust is a critical component to organizational, professional and personal relationships.

Be Happy At Work Essentials

1. A certain level of trust is needed to have a peaceful atmosphere and meet daily work goals to increase productivity.

2. Trust builds loyalty, respect and a supportive work environment.

3. Trust is critical for professional and personal relationships.

4. Build trust by maintaining direct eye contact when you speak to anyone.

5. Building trusting relationships is a process which takes time and effort from all parties.

6. The most important step in building trust is to be honest.

7. Trust can take a long time to build and maintain, but can be destroyed by a single action or miscommunication.

8. It takes time to recover from betrayed trust.

9. Watch for signs trust in eroding in your relationships and work to rebuild a high level of trust.

Chapter 3

How to Build a Strong Relationship with Your Boss

Do you celebrate your boss on National Boss or Bosses day – October 16th? National Boss Day is designated for employees to show appreciation for their managers in the U.S. and other designated countries.

Employees who have a good relationship with their boss can thank and show appreciation for encouragement, guidance and support throughout the year. Those who are not fortunate to have a good relationship can take the first step to improve the relationship on this day.

It's important to have a strong relationship with your boss throughout the year. Acknowledge your manager for help on projects, making your job easier, understanding when you need unplanned time off, responsive to your calls and emails in a timely manner, being fair and creating the best work environment possible.

On a local level invite your manager to coffee, breakfast, lunch or break which allows you to get to know your manager and vice versa. For long distance or field positions manage your relationship with your manager by dropping a "thank you" card in the mail quarterly to show your appreciation, thoughtfulness which keeps you visible. A thank you card is recommended over an email. A thank you card can be displayed on the desk as a reminder and be admired by others. When your manager spends time with you in the field make sure the time is well spent. Plan a good day in the field and use this time to build and strengthen your relationship.

Your boss holds the key to internal advancements and external career opportunities when you need a professional reference. A strong relationship allows you to understand and accomplish work objectives and goals to advance your career. Listed are strategies to improve your relationship with your boss.

Fourteen Strategies to Strengthen Your Relationship with Your Boss

1. *Think ahead.* Identify upcoming challenges your boss will encounter and offer suggested solutions. Anticipate questions which might be asked regarding a project and prepare

thoughtful answers. Thinking ahead will show you are strategic and valuable team member.

2. **Show value.** You were hired to add value to your department and organization. Bosses want employees who are not shy about speaking up and discussing business challenges which need to be addressed. Stand out by providing facts, confidence and solutions which produce results.

3. **Make your boss look good.** Make your boss look good. Do not correct your boss in the presence of other people – do this in a private setting and make sure you are right! Display a level of respect and professionalism which benefits you professionally.

4. **Know how to communicate with your boss.** When is the best time to communicate with your boss? Is your boss a morning or afternoon person? Do they prefer a short email, text or phone call? Learn how your supervisor prefers to be communicated can greatly improve your relationship.

5. **Ask for feedback.** Do not assume you are doing a great job make a point to gain feedback about your performance quarterly. Employees often shy away about asking how they are doing for fear of criticism. The good news is you can take action to improve your performance before your annual review.

6. ***Communicate on a personal level.*** Get to know your supervisor on a personal level. Find out about their hobbies, personal or community interests. You may decide to support your boss in an event to improve your relationship.

7. ***Offer to help on projects.*** Ask your supervisor if they need help on a project where your expertise may be valuable. Their calendars stay busy and full – an offer to help will inform them you are willing to take on more responsibility and position you for possible advancement.

8. ***Communicate with your boss.*** Keep your supervisor informed about the status of projects, challenges and successes. Good communication builds trust and no surprises.

9. ***Manage your workload - under promise and over deliver.*** Completing projects before the due date shows you are proactive and accountable for assignments. Waiting to the day a project is due to turn it in communicates a lack of time management and consideration for the person waiting on the project.

10. ***Ask for advice and help.*** Ask for advice and help on assignments which are important. Reach out to your co-workers for less important assignments, however be careful not to appear you are needy or can not make decisions on your own.

11. **Respect your manager.** You do not have to like your manager- but you should respect their position and understand they have the power to control your advancement.

12. **Be sincere.** Do not kiss up to your boss. Do not go out of your way to get them a cup of coffee or bring bottled water for them everyday. Be you and they will see your natural kindness.

13. **Do not gossip.** Stay away from office gossip – never engage in office gossip about your supervisor. The word tends to get out what you said not what the other person said.

14. **Establish trust and a line of communication.** You will establish trust with your supervisor by being honest. Use quality time when you are together to build trust, rapport, share work progress and have fun.

Employees who build strong relationships with their supervisors can look to them for advice and a go to person you can count on for coaching.

Be Happy At Work Essentials

1. Celebrate your boss on National Boss Day – October 16th in the U.S. and other designated countries.

2. Build strong relationship with your boss throughout the year.

3. A "thank you" card is a great way to show your appreciation for your boss.

4. Make your boss look good.

5. Manage your relationship with your boss if you expect to advance your career.

6. Know how and when the best time to communicate with your boss.

7. Ask for feedback about your performance quarterly to make improvements before your annual review.

8. Establish trust with an open line of communication.

9. Employees who have a good relationship with their boss have a better chance at career advancement.

How to Keep Your Boss Happy Managing Your Micro Manager

Does your boss micro-manage you? Do you want to take control over your work and be treated with dignity and respect? Listed are steps you can take to manage your micro-manager.

Good first impression. Make a good first impression and be consistent. When you build your manager's confidence they will less likely control every aspect of your work.

Identify wants and needs. Identify what your boss's needs and wants are and do your part to fulfill them. Does your boss seek approval from his boss or clients? Does your boss want to complete projects before the deadline? Does your boss want a promotion and will do whatever it takes to make their department look good?

Set performance objectives. Discuss your performance goals and objectives with your boss. Set goals which are achievable and realistic. Goals and objectives which are not met will lead to tighter micro-management.

Progress reports. Schedule regular on-on-one meetings with your boss to track your performance and re-assess your goals.

Open communication. When your positive performance does not change the behavior of your micro-manager communicate directly with them about your concerns. Communicate your abilities and confidence you earned to be independent. Ask if you could change anything in your performance which will increase their confidence in you.

Move on. If the micro-management style continues to smother your performance consider a career change.

No boss has control over your well being – only you do unless you give that power to them. Start to see your boss as a human being – caught in their predicament – not in control of your well being – when you do – the dynamics of the "boss" role changes. Think about things which are right about your job and spend less time thinking about what's wrong.

Be Happy At Work Essentials

1. Always make a good first impression and be consistent.

2. Identify what your boss wants and needs are and do your part to fulfill them.

3. Schedule time with your boss to discuss your performance goals.

4. Be happy you are employed and not looking for a job.

Chapter 4

Office Politics

How to Play the Office Politics Game and Win

Are you good at office politics? Office politics is essential and requires you to interact, work well and build relationships with others to get things done.

No matter now great your work is – if you do not work well in a team environment you may find yourself in a dead end job. People who play office politics get what they want within reason. Those who say nothing – get nothing in return.

Whether you want to or not it's important you play the political game to find out how your peers and other relationships are developed. Be nice to everyone – understand your strengths and how to use them to engage others.

Office politics involves the perceptions people have of you. Not all people will be easy to work with – however its how you choose to work with them will determine your political success. At work be actively engaged in building and nurturing relationships. Learn about your peers and discover their strengths, weaknesses and make genuine connections with everyone around you.

How Do You Play Politics at Work and Win?

Build Relationships

Office politics crosses all cultures and age groups. Use office politics to build relationships, accomplish work objectives to advance your career.

Build Your Social Network

Get to know politically successful people in your department and the organization. Build relationships with peers, bosses and executives. Build relationships with those who have informal power. Build your relationships on respect and trust – not flattery. Be friendly with everyone but do not align yourself with any group.

Manage Your Network

Make a list of internal and external people you need to know to advance your career. Introduce yourself to them and meet with them for breakfast, lunch, break or dinner on a regular basis.

Socialize with different people at least three times per week to build your network. Ask questions about where they went to school, how they got their job and show them you care about them. Seek advice from those you respect and trust.

1. Build multiple informal networks to gain access to departments and company information.

2. Build your brand and visibility of your achievements.

3. Improve new and difficult relationships.

4. Volunteer for career opportunities where you can shine and build your network.

5. Identify new ways to make yourself, boss and team look good.

6. Say yes to every opportunity to gain access to the right people at the right time.

Do You Have A Mentor?

Make it a priority to get to know different people within your department and organization. Seek out someone in a higher position than you and ask them to mentor you – more than likely they will be flattered you asked.

Manage Your Own Behavior

Be observant and a good listener and learn about your organization culture. Identify successful people and behaviors you can model by setting standards for yourself to avoid negative politics from spreading.

1. Do not gossip or spread rumors – when you hear something negative consider the source.

2. Do not allow yourself to be involved in arguments.

3. Maintain your integrity at all times.

4. Maintain your professionalism – career success begins with professionalism.

5. Be positive – do not complain.

6. Be confident but not overly aggressive.

7. Do not rely on confidentiality – use good judgment and decide what you should disclose.

Make Politics Work for You

Accept the reality there will be office politics and use your own social strategies to deal with day-to-day political behavior. Use information you gather to build your political network.

Who Has the Power?

Re-chart the organization – take time to watch and observe movers and shakers.

1. Who are the real influencers and who do they influence?

2. Who has the power but does not use it?

3. Who wants the power but does not have it?

4. Who is respected and trusted?

5. Who mentors and sponsors others?

Be Happy At Work Essentials

1. When you make a decision not to play the political game - you allow others who may have less knowledge, expertise and skill to influence decision makers.

2. Smart politicking will help you achieve your goals without compromising your integrity.

3. Use political power to accomplish your goals but not sabotage others.

4. Be positive at all times.

5. Be a good listener and observer.

6. Identify the movers, shakers and those who have the power and authority for you to accomplish your goals.

PART TWO

How to Get Ahead and Fast Track Your Career

Chapter 5

Career Vision, Mission and Goals

Do you have a vision for your future? Before you can get ahead at work you need a career plan of what you want to accomplish. Many people fall into a career by accident; some play it safe and remain where they landed. For those who want more control it's essential to have a career plan and set goals to measure your performance.

Have you wondered why a career and vision plan is important? A career plan increases your fulfillment and happiness. It allows you to take control and make a conscious decision about what you want instead of settling for a career you may regret later in life.

A Career Plan Will

Networking. Help you determine networking options to achieve your goals.

Skill Set. Plan time and resources you need to improve your skill set.

Technology. Help you improve your technology skills.

Personal Brand. Allow time for you to build your personal brand.

Career Path. You avoid regret of having gone down the wrong career path.

Control. Prevents internal and external events from controlling your career path.

Proactive. Guides you to be proactive instead of reacting to events you can not control. Allows you to control your destiny – not someone else.

Good Fit. Ensures a good fit for you and your work.

The Cost of Not Having a Career Plan

1. You are unhappy at work and dislike your job.

2. You are unfulfilled which has a negative impact on your work, personal relationships and your health.

3. You have a lack of personal power.

4. Your career options are limited.

5. You do not realize your career potential.

S.M.A.R.T. goal is defined as one which is specific, measurable, achievable, realistic and timely.

EXAMPLE: A general goal would be "take technology classes." A specific goal would be - take an excel class and complete it in six months.

Specific: A specific goal should be written and clearly defined by answering the following questions.

Who: Who is involved in your career plan?

What: What do you want to accomplish?

When: When is the target date to accomplish your goals?

Why: Why have you chosen these goals?

How: How do you plan to accomplish your goals?

Measurable. How will you measure your goal as evidence you have accomplished your plan? When you measure progress it allows you to stay on track and accomplish your target dates.

Achievable. Goals you set should be achievable and challenging. Goals which are achievable will motivate you to accomplish them.

Realistic. A goal must be realistic – you are the only one who can determine if your goals are set too high or low. High goals will drive and challenge you whereas low goals will not stimulate your mind. Unrealistic goals will not motive you.

Time. Goals should have a target date for completion – without a date there is no motivation to accomplish them.

You have a better chance of accomplishing your goals if they are specific, measurable, achievable, and realistic with a commitment to achieve them by a planned time.

Useful Tips and Resources

Career Coach. Consult with a career coach to provide advice for a career plan.

Books. Read self-help books for your industry.

Skill Trends. Identify skills for the future to build your brand and stand out from your peers.

Work Trends. Identify work trends which impact your career plans and future.

Career Success. Make a list of what you want from your career to be successful.

Marketable Skills. Identify how to best market your skills.

Calendar. Plan time on your calendar to create a career vision plan and review it quarterly for updates and revisions.

Professional Development. Plan financial resources to invest in personal and professional development.

Accountability. S.M.A.R.T. goals allow you to be accountable for your career.

Resume. Write your resume or curriculum vitae for three to five years.

The S.M.A.R.T goal concept is essential to accomplishing professional goals. Your goals can be linked to your department, division and future career plans.

Be Happy At Work Essentials

1. To get ahead you need a career vision and plan.

2. A career coach will help you develop a career plan.

3. S.M.A.R.T goal is defined as one which is specific, measurable, achievable, realistic and timely.

4. A career plan increases your fulfillment and happiness.

5. A career plan allows you to be proactive instead of reacting to events you can not control such as unemployment.

6. Identify skill trends for the future to build your brand to stand out from your peers.

7. A career plan and S.M.A.R.T goals allow you to be accountable for your career.

Chapter 6

How to Find a Sponsor at Work

What is a Sponsor?

A sponsor is a senior level executive who has the power and position to take your career to the top. Sponsors invest their time and take a sincere interest in your career. They provide, advice, direction and leadership skills so you can take smart calculated risks. Sponsors benefit from time invested in you for mutual career advancement which builds their brand for potential opportunities.

Do you have a sponsor? Sponsors are the new way to fast track your career. You need sponsors who have the position, influence and decision making power to transform your career to achieve your goals. You can find and introduce yourself to potential sponsors within your organization, networking events, meetings, conferences and industry meetings.

Plan your "elevator speech" – discuss your current status and background which would engage a potential sponsor in a conversation. Be prepared to discuss who you are, accomplishments, goals, why you have asked them to be your sponsor and how your relationship will benefit both parties. If your target sponsor is not available ask for a referral to someone else.

You will need more than one sponsor to get your dream job. Once your sponsors are onboard – do not use your business relationship to share your personal life secrets. Know where to draw the line in your professional relationship. Identify five potential sponsors who have the power to fast track your career.

Five Sponsor Targets

1. Sponsor Name: _____

Company: _____

Position of Power: _____

Your Goal: _____

2. Sponsor Name: _____

Company: _____

Position of Power: _____

Your Goal: _____

3. Sponsor Name: _____

Company: _____

Position of Power: _____

Your Goal: _____

4. Sponsor Name: _____

Company: _____

Position of Power: _____

Your Goal: _____

5. Sponsor Name: _____

Company: _____

Position of Power: _____

Your Goal: _____

As you gain sponsors consider introducing them to each other in person, email or teleconference – they may consider collaborating for your career success.

Three Sponsors to Avoid

1. Boss / Manager. Your boss although the intention is appreciated – you need a sponsor who is a few levels higher than your manager.

2. Personal Friends. Personal friends are not recommended as it may hinder your relationship.

3. Role Models. Some role models lack the power, influence and connections you need to advance your career.

Who Needs a Sponsor?

Are you ready to fast track your career? Every professional who is serious about their career needs a sponsor. A sponsor believes in you, your potential and will advocate for your next promotion or salary increase. A sponsor will help you develop strategic relationships with senior executives who have the power to get you to the top. Listed are the career benefits of a sponsor.

Sixteen Benefits of a Sponsor

1. *Advice.* Provides strategic career advice to position you to achieve your goals.

2. *Alliances.* Sponsors provide strategic alliances with people who can propel you into a leadership position.

3. *Believes in you.* Sponsors believe in you and your ability and go out on a limb for you.

4. *Connects.* A sponsor connects you with potential clients, customers and potential employers.

5. *Economic downturns.* During economic downturns – a sponsor is your advocate to ensure you keep your job or help you find a new one.

6. *Interest.* Sponsors take a sincere interest in promoting your career.

7. *Investment.* An investment in your career is a benefit for your sponsor.

8. *Live Your Dreams.* Sponsors fast track you so you can live your dreams.

9. *New Opportunities.* A sponsor opens the door and points you in the right direction for new career opportunities.

10. *Perception.* A sponsor expands your perception of what you can achieve and how to do it.

11. *Performance.* A sponsor provides coaching on your performance so others will see you are a top leader and candidate for a promotion.

12. *Professional Presence.* A sponsor will coach you on how to elevate your presentation skills and appearance to be appropriate for your career.

13. *Promotion.* A sponsor advocates for your next promotion.

14. *Reputation.* Sponsors publicly put their reputation on the line to allow you to achieve your goals and a higher level of employment.

15. *Risks.* Sponsors provide coverage so you can take smart calculated career risks.

16. *Senior Leaders.* A sponsor positions you to network with senior leaders.

Protégé – What's Expected of You?

Once you have a sponsor you are wearing their brand. You are expected to take the initiative to maintain regular face-to-face, email or phone communication. Your sponsor needs to be kept informed of your performance or lack of it. A lack of communication puts their brand and your career at risk. Without communication your sponsor has no idea if you are struggling, need advice or coverage for career risks. Your success is your sponsors' eye for talent – whereas your failure is their liability.

A protégé should be trustworthy, loyal, performance driven, strategic thinker, know when to ask for help and have open communication.

You should deliver above your job description and take the initiative without being told what to do.

A protégé shows acts of kindness to their sponsors by inviting them to a meal, writing a thank you note, treat them to their favorite beverage or dessert, support and participate in their personal community or work initiative. Bottom line – be consistent and do something memorable to show your appreciation for them being your sponsor.

Be Happy At Work Essentials

1. A sponsor is a senior level executive who invests their time in your career with high expectations of your performance and loyalty.

2. A sponsor is the new way to put your career on the fast track.

3. A sponsor provides career advice, guidance, develops you as a leader and provides support so you can take smart calculated risks.

4. A sponsor benefits from time invested in you for mutual career advancement.

5. You need more than one sponsor to achieve your career goals.

6. You can identify potential sponsors within your organization, at industry meetings,

networking events and conferences.

7. Sponsors build their brand as they develop you.

8. Your success is your sponsors' eye for talent – whereas your failure is their liability.

9. A protégé wears their sponsors brand in everything they do.

10. A protégé is expected to have open communication with your sponsor about your performance on a regular basis.

11. A protégé is expected to be trustworthy, loyal and performance driven.

12. A protégé shows ongoing appreciation for the support of their sponsors.

"Self-Confidence is a critical component to professional development."

- Patricia Dorch

Chapter 7

Self Confidence at Work
How to Prepare for Success

Self-confidence is what it takes to be happy. Think about someone you know who is happy they are confident in their abilities. Find someone who is unhappy chances are they lack the confidence they need to be happy in their career and personal life.

The absence of confidence prevents you from accomplishing all life has to offer you. Self-confidence will remove the barrier for you to achieve your career and life goals. Although you will face challenges – confidence in your ability to learn, be adaptable and grow is essential.

Build Self-Confidence

Thirteen Secrets to Improve Your Confidence

1. **Achievements**. Prepare an "achievements list" and go back as far as you would like. Once you make a list add new achievements. Everyday review your list of achievements to remind yourself how good you are and what you have accomplished.

   For example: If you are good at purchasing products and services add "purchasing expert" to your list.

2. **Believe in Yourself.** Tell yourself you can achieve what you want – then believe it!

3. **Challenge.** Volunteer for projects to increase confidence, use your strengths and learn new skills. Stay focused and do not compare yourself with others.

4. **Contribution.** Make a contribution by volunteering for a company or community event. Check your company website for "community initiatives" and get involved. Participating in something new can build your confidence in other areas of your career and life.

5. **Dress Professional.** When you look good you feel good. Be conscious of your personal appearance. When you don't look good it changes how you feel and how others interact with you. Buy quality clothing which last longer and look better on you.

6. **Knowledge.** Review your work goals and identify skills you need to improve. Consider taking an online course, seminar or participating in your organization online professional development classes. These strategies provide a certificate of achievement which you can add to your list and resume.

7. **Mindset.** Get yourself in the right mindset. Think about where you are now, where you want to go and what steps are required for you to be successful.

8. **Positive Self-Talk.** Tell yourself you can do what it takes to achieve your goals. Do not allow negative thoughts to discourage you from achieving your goals. Controlling your thoughts and concentrating on positive self-talk increases self-confidence.

9. **Sit Up Front.** Do you go to the back of the room at meetings, conferences, training and other events? People prefer the back of the room as a way of not being seen. Going to the back of the room reflects a lack of confidence to sit up front in the company of movers and shakers.

10. **Speak Up.** Do you speak up at meetings and during group discussions? Many people never speak up because they fear people will judge them based on what they say. People tend to be more accepting of ideas than you think. Speaking up builds your self-confidence, public speaking skills and you gain respect from management and your peers who see you as a leader.

11. **Success.** Stretch yourself beyond your comfort zone to build self-confidence and put you on a path to success.

12. **Uniqueness.** Embrace your uniqueness - there is no reason for you to compare yourself to anyone else. Decide what you want and create a plan of action to succeed.

13. **S.W.O.T. Career Analysis.** S.W.O.T stands for Strengths, Weaknesses, Opportunities and Threats.

What are your strengths, weaknesses, opportunities to develop new or improved skills and threats? Make a plan to improve your weaknesses and threats which limit your success. Take a moment to identify your S.W.O.T Career Analysis.

S.W.O.T. Career Analysis

Strengths – What are your strengths?

1. _____
2. _____
3. _____
4. _____
5. _____

Weaknesses – What skills do you need to add or improve?

1. _____
2. _____
3. _____
4. _____
5. _____

Opportunities – What new career opportunities can you pursue with your current skills?

1. _____
2. _____
3. _____
4. _____
5. _____

Threats -What prevents you from achieving your goals and what is your plan to remove them as threats?

1. _____
2. _____
3. _____
4. _____
5. _____

Be Happy At Work Essentials

Self-confidence is important in every area of your career and life. People who do not have self-confidence find it difficult to become successful and happy.

1. Self-confidence will remove the barrier for you to achieve career and life goals.

2. An "achievement list" will build your self-confidence.

3. Believe in yourself – tell yourself you can achieve what you want – then believe it!

4. Make a contribution by volunteering to build your confidence.

5. S.W.O.T. Career Analysis will identify your strengths, weaknesses, opportunities and threats.

6. Talk to yourself in a way which is positive.

7. Speak up at meetings, training, conferences and events to build self-confidence and public speaking skills.

8. Self-confidence at work will lead to a high level of career success and happiness.

Chapter 8

New Habits of
Highly Successful People

Whether you are an experienced professional or newcomer there are common habits top performers use to approach work. Employees who practice good work habits establish a successful career with an employer, get things done to position for a raise or promotion. During your performance review management will assess how effective and productive you are for their organization. Use these new habits to increase your productivity and perform at your peak.

New Habits of
Highly Successful People

1. *Accountable.* Are you accountable for your work? Be accountable for work in your job description and get it done in a timely manner.

2. *Attention to Detail.* Do you follow directions and give attention to detail? When your employer gives specific instructions on an assignment it's expected you follow the instructions and pay attention to detail. Top performers complete assignments before its due date and provide accurate details. Sloppy work is unacceptable and will get you noticed for the wrong reasons. You are not hurting your employer – you are hurting your career.

3. *Follow-up.* When you send an email about a project, report, meeting or presentation – follow-up as a courtesy reminder. Follow-up skills provide time for discussions, revisions, meet deadlines and preparation required to achieve goals.

4. *Initiative.* Do you take the initiative to get work done? Do not wait to be told what to do - take the initiative to get work done and help your peers who might need assistance.

5. *Interpersonal Skills.* Be friendly and have a positive attitude towards your peers and management. Do not walk around with a bad attitude, long face; make sarcastic remarks when things do not go your way. Keep your voice upbeat when you are on the telephone – how you speak is a reflection of you and the organization you represent.

6. *Know What Work is.* Although checking emails are important – spend time

accomplishing tasks which require focus and productivity.

7. *Manage your Time.* Keep a time log of how long it takes to complete specific projects and reports. New projects tend to take longer than those you do weekly, monthly and quarterly. Be conscious of how you spend your time.

8. *Organized.* What does your work station communicate to others about you? Manage what people see in your work area – keep your desk, in basket, bookshelves, files and mobile office organized. Your workstation or mobile office should be neat, clean and have a pleasant odor.

9. *Plan for Success.* Identify tasks and projects which you can complete in a timely manner and allow more time for projects and reports which require focus and assistance.

10. *Planning Sessions.* Have weekly planning sessions to determine how you will spend your time to stay on track and accomplish goals.

11. *Practice your Job Skills.* Ask your manager for constructive feedback to improve and develop new skills before your next performance review.

12. *Priority.* Identify what's important and what can wait. Set priorities to meet all deadlines

before the target date will allow time for revisions and unexpected emergencies.

13. Problem Solve. Are you a problem solver? Identify problems, determine specific actions and consult with others for the best solutions.

14. Punctual. Are you punctual? How you start your day will impact the rest of your day – start early to be relaxed and on time.

15. Responsibility. Know your job description and take responsibility for what's expected of you.

16. Sleep. A good night sleep will allow you to maintain focus, confidence and perform at the highest level.

17. Teamwork. Be a team player. Share your ideas, information and work experiences with your peers. In a competitive work environment - do not share your career capital – skills which are unique to you.

Be Happy At Work Essentials

1. Be accountable and responsible for work outlined in your job description.

2. Complete all assignments on time in a professional manner.

3. Take the initiative to get work done – do not wait to be told what to do.

4. Know the difference between work and busy work.

5. Spend time improving and learning new skills.

6. A good night sleep has everything to do with your performance and how you interact with others.

New habits empower top performers to increase productivity, the bottom line, get promoted and be happy at work.

Chapter 9

Create Visibility

The Power of Personal Branding – A Career Distinction Tool

Do you sit quietly all year with your head down? Do you work hard to build your personal brand to become visible and "stand out" from your peers? A personal brand is a "career distinction" which identifies and differentiates you from other peers and colleagues in your industry with similar knowledge, skills and abilities.

It's essential to discuss your career plans and with your manager who can have an active role in providing advice, and exposure you need to achieve your career goals. Create visibility by using these steps to build your personal brand within your organization and industry.

Twenty One Steps to Build Your Personal Brand

Step 1: Accomplishments. Keep a list of your accomplishments and emails you receive acknowledging a job well done. Be sure your achievements are not overlooked during your performance review – it's not the responsibility of your manager to remember what you have achieved.

Step 2: Build Strong Internal Relationships. Build strong internal relationships with your immediate supervisor, management and peers. Seek out new relationships in other departments such as information technology, human resources, sales, marketing, purchasing and other departments you might have an interest in the future.

Take the initiative to invite new contacts to lunch, break and social hour after work. Do not consistently have lunch with the same people – you limit building new relationships which is essential to your success. A large internal network and alliance will allow you to build new relationships.

Step 3: Career Distinction. What is your career distinction? Think of yourself as a brand – what makes brand "you" unique from brand x – your peers and competition?

1. _____

2. _____

3. _____

4. _____

5. _____

Personal Brand. What is your personal brand strategy to "stand out" from others?

1. _____

2. _____

3. _____

Strengths. What are your top five strength?

1. _____

2. _____

3. _____

4. _____

5. _____

How will you use your strengths to achieve your goals?

_____
_____
_____
_____
_____

Professional Development. What is your professional development plan to improve your personal brand?

_____
_____
_____
_____
_____

Attributes. What are your top five attributes and how do you plan to use them to build your personal brand?

Top Five Attributes:

1. _____

2. _____

3. _____

4. _____

5. _____

Plans:

_____

_____

_____

_____

_____

Certifications. Consider certifications, certificates or an advanced degree to position your brand distinction.

Step 4: Career Investment. Career investment is an ongoing process which enhances your brand. Increase your knowledge, skills; expand your network to sell your brand for internal promotions and external new career opportunities.

- Read books, articles and blogs and subscribe to newsletters which relate to your industry.

- Attend seminars to increase industry knowledge.

- Teach a class at a college or university to network and gain recognition for your brand.

- Do not settle for where you are – make a commitment for life-long learning.

Step 5: Expand Your Horizon. Get involved in projects within your division to gain exposure and open new career doors.

Step 6: Industry Expert. Become recognized as an industry expert – speak at conferences, trade shows and universities.

Step 7: Interact with Top Management. Look for ways to interact with top management at meetings and conferences. Wear your name badge so others can put a face with a name. Volunteer for projects and committees to meet and interact with executives.

Step 8: Loyalty. Your reputation for loyalty will follow you throughout your career and impact your personal brand. People who can influence others about your loyalty are:

- Clients
- Colleagues
- Competition
- Co-workers
- Customers
- Employers
- Industry contacts
- Military Contacts

Step 9: Networks. Identify and join internal networks organized by your employer.

Build networks with industry contacts which are in the same field to gain introductions.

Step 10: One-on-One Meetings with your Manager. Schedule regular one-on-one meetings with your manager. If you are in a field or remote position schedule a bi-weekly teleconference to check on your performance. Prepare a short agenda for your manager to discuss past projects and current assignments. Ask about recommendations for improvements and advice to learn new skills.

Step 11: Positioning. Position your brand to be seen and heard by influential people in your industry. Be known as someone who has an engaging personality, respected and trusted resource for industry advice. Be conscious of your business etiquette, mannerisms, and manners which are observed by others.

Step 12: Power of Reputation. A good reputation is earned by brand management. Your reputation should add value in your area of expertise. Employers want to be associated with a brand which is unique and has a strong reputation.

Seek feedback from co-workers, colleagues, friends, military contacts and industry experts to determine how others perceive your personal brand. Use feedback to evaluate your brand to be successful.

Visit social websites regularly to monitor and protect your reputation to make a good impression to employers.

Step 13: Power of Thank-you in Business. A thank-you note is a powerful business tool and gesture of professional courtesy. The regular practice of writing a thank-you note will help you be remembered which enhances your personal brand.

Write a thank-you note to co-workers, managers, interviewers and others. Although an email thank-you lacks formality – it can be used when time is an issue or email is the best method of communicating. Show gratitude and appreciation by using two simple words "thank-you" which has the power to transform your career.

Writing a thank-you note is the easiest and most powerful strategy you can use to achieve success. A thank-you card can be displayed on a desk as a reminder of your appreciation and admired by other professionals.

A thank-you note shows your personal brand, business etiquette, appreciation and professionalism. Never underestimate the power of a thank-you note - it never goes without being noticed.

Step 14: Practice. If you plan to speak at a meeting or event take time to prepare notes and practice your presentation. Practice out loud to hear how you sound and continue to practice until you are confident in your presentation. Anticipate you will have questions and how to respond and overcome concerns without being defensive. If time allows present your presentation to a co-worker or manager who can provide constructive feedback.

Step 15: Responsibility. Take responsibility – ask your manager how you can make a contribution to your team. Volunteer to be on a committee and attend meetings to represent your team and department. An employee who is known is better than one who is unknown.

Step 16: Self-Promotion. Do not be afraid of self promotion wear your name badge at all times.

Step 17: Showcase your Skills. Seminars and meetings are a great place to showcase your skills to your manager and co-workers and colleagues. These opportunities provide a platform for you to gain exposure and share your knowledge.

Step 18: Sponsor. Identify a sponsor in your company who can assist you in achieving your career goals.

Step 19: Take Action – Right Now! Become visible right now. Do not wait until tomorrow or when you feel more confident – start today.

Step 20: Visibility Campaign. The most effective way to increase your visibility is to get your name out in the industry. Establish a visibility campaign by:

- Maintaining and expanding your internal and external network with co-workers, colleagues, clients, customers, friends and industry contacts.

- Attend and speak at industry conferences, meetings and participate in industry panel discussions.

- Write an online book review on a topic which relates to your industry – this becomes part of your online identity when people search your name.

- Write an online blog- become known as an industry expert on a topic of your expertise to showcase your work.

Step 21: Visual Brand – Appearance. Your visual brand sends a non-verbal message about your success. What does your visual brand say about you?

Make a powerful visual impression and be consistent with your appearance. Reinforce your personal brand by aligning your appearance with your unique promise of value.

- Wear signature accessories.

- Your body language, gestures and posture all communicate your personal brand.

- Your visual brand should communicate success.

- How distinct is your visual brand from others?

- Do others perceive your visual brand as positive or does it need work?

- Is your visual brand memorable? What makes you stand out?

- What steps can you take to improve your visual brand?

Personal branding is building a brand personality which is your personal and intellectual assets used to differentiate you from others. Whether you are seeking a promotion, new job or Military to Civilian Transition – build your brand and career distinction. Communicate your unique promise of value to internal or external potential employers. Manage your brand reputation, visual brand, platform, online presence and brand community.

Today every career advantage counts – use innovative personal branding strategies as a career distinction to stand out in any economy or industry.

Be Happy At Work Essentials

1. A personal brand is a "career distinction" which differentiates you from your peers and colleagues in your industry.

2. What is your brand strategy to "stand-out" from others?

3. A career investment is an ongoing process to enhance your brand.

4. Wear your name badge at all times.

5. Become known and recognized as an expert in your industry.

6. Identify internal networks organized by your company and new networks you can build.

7. Schedule one-on-one meetings with your manager to provide feedback about your performance.

8. A good reputation is earned by brand management which follows you throughout your career.

9. Visit social websites to monitor your brand reputation.

10. A "thank-you" note is a powerful business tool.

11. It takes practice, practice, practice to be good at public speaking.

12. Personal branding allows you to stand out in any economy and industry

Chapter 10

Career Capital

How to Build Career Capital and Succeed at Work

What is career capital? Career capital is your portfolio of work – it's your unique experiences, knowledge, skills, personality and attributes which set you apart from others. Career capital enables you to produce financial value, be visible, find a job, get promoted and create new situations for your future. Professionals make "skill deposits" to build their portfolio, platform and career capital account. Learn how to build your career capital by using these secret strategies.

Twenty Secret Strategies to
Build Career Capital

Strategy 1: Improve your Skills and Adopt New Ones. Take professional development courses in your industry. Participate in online courses at your company to receive a certificate of achievement. Ask your mentor for advice about what they would recommend you need to accomplish your career goals in three, five or ten years from now.

Strategy 2: Develop a Career Portfolio. Write articles which people want to read about in your industry. The good news about writing is once your articles are on the internet – they speak for you – twenty four hours per day.

Strategy 3: Build a Network of People. Build a network of people you know and those who can be valuable for the future. Introduce colleagues to people who can be helpful and provide references for them. Real career capital comes from helping others become successful.

Strategy 4: Make Skill Deposits in Your Career Capital Account. Career capital is not achieved overnight or with one organization however, what you build will be with you always. The skills you deposit in your account will boost your value and career options over the long-term.

Strategy 5: Return the Favor. When people help you return the favor by helping them or someone in their network. You may be asked to volunteer time in a community charity event or introduction to someone in your network.

Strategy 6: Propose a New Idea or Project. Pitch an idea or project which can be valuable to your department or organization. Do your research and discuss your ideas with your manager. Be prepared to provide who, what, when, where and how and overcome objections or concerns with good answers. Be open to ideas which might work well with your proposal – any partial or full acceptance of the proposal creates a skill deposit in your career capital account.

Strategy 7: Attend Industry Events. Attend events and arrive early to meet new people and build your network. Volunteer to be on a conference committee is a great way to gain visibility and meet people of influence.

Strategy 8: Learn New Skills. Writing an article for your industry is a unique way to become a subject expert. Media interviews provide the exposure you need to increase your career options.

Strategy 9: Industry Journals. Reading industry journals provides topics of conversation at industry functions and increases your career capital.

Strategy 10: Adapt a Skill Mindset. What top skills can you offer which has economic value and allow you to advance and make career capital deposits?

Skills:

1. _____

2. _____

3. _____

Strategy 11: Valuable Skills. Identify skills which are valuable for your industry and success. Network with people who have skills you need and ask advice about how you might achieve them.

Strategy 12: Mental Discomfort. Do not allow yourself to get comfortable with your current skills – stretch yourself to learn something new.

Strategy 13: Seek Honest Feedback. Honest feedback might seem harsh – however you will discover skills you need to enhance and how to use the skills you have for the future.

Strategy 14: Quality Time. Spend quality time on activities which enable you to grow and reduce time spent on those which do not.

Strategy 15: Work With A Goal in Mind. Do work which allows you to accomplish goals and avoid doing "busy" work.

Strategy 16: Patience. Be patient learning new skills which may take months or years to acquire for the future.

Strategy 17: Contributions. Volunteering will allow you to build career capital and make a contribution.

Strategy 18: Industry Experience. Industry experience provides access to internal and external networks in your company and community.

Strategy 19: Write Articles. Write industry articles and submit them to article websites – to be visible on the internet.

Strategy 20: The Big Payoff. Career capital allows you to offer real value and leverage your career options to increase your financial goals.

CAREER CAPITAL ACCOUNT

WHAT ARE YOUR TOP SKILLS?

1. _____

2. _____

3. _____

4. _____

5. _____

6. _____

7. _____

8. _____

9. _____

10. _____

CAREER CAPITAL DEPOSITS

WHAT SKILLS DO YOU NEED TO ADD TO YOUR ACCOUNT?

Skill Deposits   **Target Date**

1. _____

2. _____

3. _____

4. _____

5. _____

6. _____

7. _____

8. _____

9. _____

10. _____

Be Happy At Work Essentials

1. Career capital is your portfolio of work – it's your unique experiences, knowledge, skills, personality and attributes which set you apart from others.

2. Highly successful people make "skill deposits" to improve existing skills and adopt new ones.

3. Your career capital account can not be achieved overnight – or with one organization.

4. What skills can you offer which have economic value?

5. Honest feedback allows you to discover skills you need to enhance and ones you need to add to your career capital account.

6. Be patient when learning new skills which are valuable for your future.

7. Career capital allows you to leverage your career options to increase financial goals.

Chapter 11

Smart Career Risks Can Boost Your Performance

Are you a risk taker? If you want to achieve anything great in your career or life – there will be risks. Many people fear taking risk the initial step needed to move out of their comfort zone to pursue a career or life style which is more rewarding.

As with any risk you stand to lose money, time and your reputation. However, the benefits of taking risks can bring positive experiences and results to provide a happier career, life and rewards.

Risk Taking Rewards

1. *New Challenges and Opportunities.* Taking risks allows you to experience new challenges and career opportunities. Learn new skills such as public speaking, presentation skills, sales, or a new technology skill.

2. *New Boundaries.* Risks empower you to expand your thinking and set new boundaries to improve your ability to achieve new levels of success.

3. *Creativity.* Risks allows you to be creative, access skills you need to problem solve, think on your feet and use ideas and resources.

4. *Positive Outcomes.* There are no perfect plans for positive outcomes. You will never know if you can succeed unless you take risks. The reward of taking risks can have positive outcomes when you have done your best to achieve your goals.

5. *Calculated Risks.* Calculated risks require a plan, careful thought and goals. By taking risks you accomplish career and life goals – the reward.

Be Happy At Work Essentials

1. If you want to achieve anything great in your career and life there will always be risks.

2. The benefits of taking risks can bring positive rewards.

3. New risks empower you to expand your thinking and set new boundaries.

4. Risk-taking allows you to be creative.

5. You will never know if you can succeed unless you take risks.

6. Calculated risks require a plan, careful thought and goals.

7. Risk-taking provides happiness when you achieve your goals.

Trust your instincts and facts to guide you through the decision making process of risks you pursue. You will never know what you can achieve unless you take smart calculated risks with no guarantees. Risks provide new challenges, outlooks and increased self-confidence. No risk – No reward.

Chapter 12

How to Position Yourself for a Promotion

Do you want a promotion but afraid to ask? Have you received consistent positive feedback about how well you perform on the job? Does your performance reviews show you "exceed" not "meet" expectations? If you answered yes to these questions it's time to ask for a promotion or title change. Use these steps to plan for a promotion.

Nine Steps to Position Yourself for a Promotion Before You Ask

Step 1: Establish Work Goals. Ask your manager about specific goals or objectives you are expected to accomplish which should be in writing. Create an action plan which clearly defines your performance expectations.

Establish target dates to "check-in" with your manager to assess your progress.

Step 2: Volunteer to Work on Projects. Volunteering provides exposure to new skills, departments and company executives.

Step 3: Be Accountable. Be accountable for your work and actions. For example – if you are working on a project and over budget be accountable for the results. Discuss with your manager a plan to solve a future problem and better outcome.

Step 4: Before you Ask. Before you ask for a promotion be sure your performance exceeds your job description. For example – you have consistently increased sales by a large percent each quarter over the last two years or you have reduced purchasing costs for your department.

Step 5: Do More! Challenge Yourself to Do More. Employees who ask for more work – take on additional responsibilities are likely to move up faster than those who only do their job description.

Why should you get a promotion? Plan your promotion strategy by identifying your top skills and how to sell them to your manager.

Step 6: Sell Your Value. What's in it for them? Sell your manager on how valuable you are to the department and organization and specifically present contributions you have made to the bottom line.

Step 7: Ask for a Meeting. During your meeting confidently explain to your manager why you have earned a promotion. For example – you are already doing the job or parts of the job assigned to another person. Never say you "deserve" a promotion.

Step 8: Show confidence and enthusiasm. Be confident and show your enthusiasm for the promotion or title change.

Step 9: Tell Why You Love Your Job. Tell your manager what the promotion or title change means to you and be sure they understand you are not adding the title change to your resume as leverage to leave the organization.

Be Happy At Work Essentials

1. Establish work goals and expectations with your manager.

2. Volunteer to work on projects to gain exposure to top executives and build your network.

3. Before you ask for a promotion or title change – be sure you are going above your job description.

4. Sell management on why you have earned a promotion or title change.

5. Tell why you love your job and the organization.

Chapter 13

Have You Earned A Raise?

How to Evaluate Your Performance

Before You Ask for a Raise

Do you want a raise? Have you thought about asking your manager for a raise based on your performance at work? Although you may think you deserve a raise – the decision to increase your salary is based on your performance and track record of success.

Before you ask for a raise consider an honest self-evaluation to assess your performance. Based on your last performance review there may be areas which need improvement and a plan to exceed expectations.

Self Evaluation

Have You Earned a Raise?

Expectations. Do you meet or exceed the expectations of your job on your last performance review? If you "meet" expectations what are the top five things you can do to exceed your performance.

Five Things I can do today:

1. _____

2. _____

3. _____

4. _____

5. _____

Reputation. Do you have a reputation for getting things done and on time? Do you push the envelope by turning in reports or assignments at the last minute? Are you consistently late? Did you know these factors impact your performance and salary increase? Do you need improvement in this area? Circle one.

1. Yes   2. No

Responsibility. Do you ask for more responsibility outside of your job description? Do you do more than what is expected of you? If you do not take on more responsibility you are limiting yourself to where you are now. Do more – get more. Circle one.

1. Yes   2. No

Leadership. Do your peers look to you for advice and leadership? Do you make yourself available to help others? Do you take a leadership role in meetings and when new hires come aboard? Do you volunteer to work on projects? You need to be seen as a leader by your manager to get a raise. Are you a leader? Circle one.

1. Yes   2. No

Knowledge. Staying on top of industry news shows your commitment and desire to be successful in your field. Do you increase your knowledge on the job and industry? Do you subscribe to industry newsletters, read industry periodicals and share your knowledge with management and your peers? Circle one.

1. Yes   2. No

New Skills. Have you improved or added new skills to your career portfolio based on your last performance review? What skills do you need or should improve to exceed performance expectations and be more marketable for internal positions? New Skills Needed:

1. _____

2. _____

3. _____

4. _____

5. _____

Accountable. Are you accountable for your work? Do you complete work assigned to you? Do you have to be reminded by your manager to complete your work? Be honest – is this an area which needs improvement? Circle one.

1. Yes   2. No

Do You Get Along Well With Others? Are you well liked by your peers? Do your co-workers want to talk to you or do they avoid you? Circle one.

1. Talk   2. Avoid

Track Record. Do you have a track record of success? Does your manager's boss know who you are and your achievements? A raise will need to be approved by him or her. If you manager's boss only knows your name – this may mean you have not done enough to stand out from your peers. Circle one.

1. I have a track record of success

2. I need to improve this area

Financial Contributions. What financial contributions have you made to your department which has reduced costs or increased revenue? Any new ideas – products or services which have been implemented? Document ideas and contributions you made which are implemented – this provides leverage for a raise. List your contributions.

1. _____

2. _____

3. _____

4. _____

5. _____

Great Job! Do you have emails which say "great job" or "well done" which speaks to your performance? You will need these emails to make your case for a raise.

Leverage. What leverage can you present today to justify a raise or increase in your salary?

1. _____

2. _____

3. _____

4. _____

5. _____

Based on the results of your self-evaluation you can determine if your performance qualifies for a raise. If more work needs to be done share your career goals with your manager; ask for advice about skills to improve, implement a plan of action and meet on a regular basis to monitor your performance. It's more difficult to ask for a raise than for it to be given to you by your employer.

Be Happy At Work Essentials

1. Before you ask for a raise – consider a self-evaluation of your performance.

2. Do you ask for more responsibility outside of your job description?

3. Have you improved or added new skills to your portfolio?

4. What financial contributions have you made to reduce costs or increase revenue?

5. What can you use as leverage based on your performance to ask for a raise?

Chapter 14

Real Money

How to Ask for a Raise

Before you ask for a raise there are essential steps you should take to prepare for the big day. Use these steps to be successful in asking for a raise.

Eight Steps to Ask for a Raise

1. *Know Your Worth.* When you ask for a raise prepare a list of accomplishments and contributions to present at your meeting. For example – if you recommended a new product or service idea, increased sales or reduced cost bring your documentation of your contribution.

2. *Know the Exact Raise You Want.* A typical raise can range from 4-10 percent per year

depending on your employer. Do salary and job description research to determine what the market is paying for someone with your achievements. Your employer will respect the fact you know what you want.

3. *Market Research.* Collect market research to present what competitors pay their employees in the same or similar role to strengthen your case. If there is no market research to support your raise request you will know before you ask for a raise.

4. *Have You Earned A Raise?* Tell why you have "earned" a raise rather than deserve a raise. Never tell an employer you deserve more money – it's what you can do for your employer and the value you add to the bottom line.

5. *Practice Asking for a Raise.* The more you practice the better you will be at getting what you want. You should not feel uncomfortable asking for what you want – a lack of confidence during your presentation can work against you.

6. *Sell Yourself.* Asking for a raise is selling your accomplishments with facts and figures. Have a category in your presentation called "exceed expectations" and present those things which make you shine.

7. *Never Threaten to Leave the Company.* Never give your employer an ultimatum about your request for a raise. If you receive your request chances are they will be interviewing for your replacement without your knowledge.

8. *What Are Your Managers Goals?* Do you know what your managers' goals are? Do you need to increase sales, create a new product or service idea, reduce production costs or distribute products to other stores faster? How can your performance help your manager achieve their goals?

Eleven Tips to Enhance Your Presentation

1. *Dress for Success.* Image is everything!

2. *Resume.* Provide an updated copy of your resume with your current position and achievements.

3. *Cover Letter.* Write a short cover letter and thank your manager for their time.

4. *Research.* Provide copies of salary and job description research.

5. *Practice.* Practice your presentation several times out loud before the big day.

6. *Be Prepared.* Be prepared if your manager has invited their manager and a human resources

representative to your presentation – this could be a good sign – don't blow it!

7. *Copies.* Have at least three sets of handouts not including your copy.

8. *Stand.* Stand when you present your presentation – this gives you power and confidence.

9. *Questions?* At the end of your presentation – ask if there are any questions or information you need to clarify. The more information you provide in your presentation the less questions you will possibly have.

10. *Close.* Close the presentation by stating – "Based on what I have presented today would you have any objection to giving me a (*state the amount*) raise?" Remain silent until your manager or another person responds. Silence is powerful. Address any questions or concerns without being defensive. Ask when a decision will be made regarding your request.

11. *Thank you.* Thank your manager and others for the opportunity to present your information.

Be Happy At Work Essentials

1. Know your worth and prepare a list of your accomplishments.

2. Know why you have earned a raise.

3. Know the exact raise you want and why.

4. Never threaten to leave the company if you do not get the raise or amount you want.

5. Practice your presentation several times out loud before you present to your manager and others.

Chapter 15

Bad Habits Can Cost Your Happiness at Work

Are you guilty of bad habits? Could one or more bad habits be affecting your performance and happiness? Do you have a social media addiction? Do you hastily respond to emails without thinking or re-reading it before you hit send? Do you post work matters or a disagreement with your employer on social media websites? A word of warning – bad work habits can cost your happiness, reduces productivity and can cost you your job.

Work Habits Can Cost You Your Job

Attitude. Rethink your attitude – are you holding on to old ways things are done? Are you resisting change because this was the way it was always done? No matter what the state of the economy avoid standing your ground, be adaptable, contribute new ideas and get along with everyone.

Be on time. Do you constantly run late for work, arrive to meetings or return from break or lunch late? Such behavior displays an attitude of carelessness. Show you are conscious and care about your job and company – be on time.

Body language. Do you roll your eyes when you are not in agreement in what you are doing, hearing or seeing? Do you avoid direct eye contact? These non-verbal communications are career killers – your actions speak louder than words. Co-workers, managers and clients interpret your non-verbal communication habits as rude and unprofessional. These behavior patterns can impact your performance and advancement.

Communication skills. Do you respond to all emails? Are you rude or abrupt in written or verbal communication? If you have a bad habit of not reading or responding to emails you could miss important messages, deadlines and be seen as unprofessional.

Company Culture. What is your company culture? Do you participate in social events? Whether your work environment is formal or informal you should observe and adhere to the company culture. Failure to "fit in" could cause tension; you could be seen as different and less desirable for the organization.

Etiquette and manners. When you ask for or receive something do you say "please" or "thank you"? If you interrupt someone say "excuse me." During a meal do you close your mouth when you chew? Do not underestimate the power of etiquette and manners in the workplace they are important for your career.

Grammar. Do you use poor grammar or slang at work? Use good grammar to avoid "word traps" in your vocabulary which show a lack of professionalism and limits your career opportunities.

Ineffective. Do you waste time, talk too much or appear to be busy but not accomplishing much? Spend time being organized and work on tasks which contribute to your productivity and the bottom line.

Lack of Assertiveness. Are your peers getting ahead of you with raises and promotions? Are you working hard to complete your assignments but your boss does not notice you? Learn to speak up about your work, successes, presentations and ideas. The person who gets promoted is not necessarily the one who does the best work. Be visible, speak up and have a take charge attitude.

Lack of Presentation Skills. Are you confident when you present to your manager and peers? You need good presentation skills to effectively communicate your message and be successful. Good content and presentation skills are your keys to success.

Negative. Do you have a habit of complaining about everything? Do people avoid you? When people avoid you – it's too late to make a change. If you have concerns speak with your manager or peers – do not attempt to gather support from others to make your point.

Office Politics. Do you kiss up to management? Are you a trouble maker – stirring the pot? Do you spread office gossip? Do your work and avoid negative distractions which damage your reputation. Your reputation will always speak for you and follow you.

Social Media on the Job. Do you have a habit of spending company time on social media or unauthorized websites? Some companies monitor the time you spend on these websites without your knowledge while others block the websites. Spending time on websites not related to or authorized by your company can cost you your job.

Independent. Although working independently is important there are times when you are expected to work with others.

Teamwork. Do you work well with others? Some people do exceptionally well on their own but shy away from working with others. Teamwork allows you to share ideas, successes and failures. If you are not seen as a team player when you have a problem to solve you may not get the support you need or the promotion you want.

Think Before You Speak. If you don't think before you speak – saying the wrong thing in an email or in person can be a career limiting move.

Time Management. Do you manage your time or do you procrastinate in getting things done? Do not put off projects or assignments until the day or hour it's due. If your last minute habit causes your manager or peers to rush this could anger your manager and hurt your relationship with your peers.

If a project fails or was not completed on time you will be the first to blame. Allow adequate time for review and revisions. When you have a report to complete the person you are sending it to will need your information in a report they need to submit to someone else.

To Tell the Truth. Misrepresenting your degree, credentials, billable hours, time card, business expenses, abusing the company credit or gas cards and others can cost you your job. It may seem as if you are getting away with it – however someone is always watching and evaluating information you submit. When there is enough evidence management will discuss it with you to confirm what you have done.

Any of these habits can cost you your job. Re-evaluate habits which put your career at risk and make a plan to improve them without allowing them to steal your happiness at work.

For more information about professional habits in the workplace I recommend my book: *Professionalism: New Rules for Workplace Career Success*.

Visit: www.whatisprofessionalism.com

Visit: www.amazon.com and barnesandnoble. com

Happy At Work Essentials

1. Rethink your attitude and avoid "standing your ground" in the workplace.

2. Be on time – show you are responsible, care about your job and respect company time.

3. Non-verbal communication – negative body language can be a career killer. Your action speaks louder than your words.

4. Do not underestimate the power of good manners and etiquette in the workplace.

5. Speak up about your work, successes, presentations and ideas.

6. You need good presentations skills to be successful at work.

7. Unauthorized time on social media and websites not related to work will cost you your job.

8. Think before your speak – saying the wrong thing in an email or face-to-face can be a career limiting move.

PART THREE

Personal and Professional
Accountability

Chapter 16

The Power of Introverts

How Your Strengths Can Get You Noticed at Work

Are you an introvert? Our business culture often favor those who are extroverts compared to those who may be considered introverts. Introverts spend a lot of time thinking and processing information.

It may be difficult for an introvert to communicate with others in person, adjust to noise levels, be a team player and make presentations – all essential skills required in the workplace. Introverts can minimize weaknesses by focusing on their knowledge and strengths. Listed are tips for introverts to excel in a collaborative workplace.

Ask Great Questions. At meetings take time to ask questions to identify what's important to your company. Good questions allow you to interact with your manager and co-workers on a small scale.

Be a Good Listener. Introverts have the ability to be good listeners and leaders. Good listeners take team ideas an implement them to achieve company goals.

Build A Strong Internal and External One-on-One Network. Introverts can build strong internal relationships with management and co-workers one person at a time rather than in large networking groups. A one-on-one relationship allows you to manage the situation and be successful.

Excel at Tasks Which Require Less Face Time. Introverts are good at assignments which require focus, attention to detail and analysis. By doing tasks which require these skills you will be noticed by your manager.

Form Connections. Throughout the day allow time to connect with co-workers instead of being alone. Use break and lunch time to connect and build existing and new individual relationships.

Know Your Worth. Knowing what you are worth will help you get the promotion you want. Use a journal to document achievements and have them available when it's time for a promotion.

Let Your Work – Get You Noticed. The impact of exceptional work and attention to detail will allow you to be visible by your manager and other executives in the organization.

Prepare for the Discomfort Zone. Are you uncomfortable when you need to give a presentation? If so, research your topic, plan and practice your presentation out loud as many times as necessary to build your confidence. Your manager and co-workers will recognize your hard work and knowledge you share.

Quite Time. When you feel stressed or overwhelmed find a quiet place where you can re-group and focus on the next step. Quite time might include taking a short walk during break or lunch to get re-energized.

Strategically Take Credit for Your Work. Strategically mention your contributions and value of your skills at the right time without bragging.

Social Media. Use social media to introduce yourself and build professional relationships with those in your field.

Be Happy At Work Essentials

1. Maximize your strengths by using them to become visible.

2. Speak up at meetings and ask great questions. Speaking up allows you to interact with management and co-workers and be seen as an active participant.

3. Build strong relationships with management and make them aware of your specific contributions.

4. Strategically promote your assets rather than assume people will see your skills and abilities.

5. Build internal and external networks by making connections with people in your industry.

6. Sign up for professional development courses and focus on areas you can improve for career advancement.

Chapter 17

How to Speak Well

Public Speaking is Important to Your Career and Income

Are you a confident public speaker? Does your lack of public speaking skills hold you back from achieving your goals? Since public speaking skills can not be avoided in the workplace look at speaking to groups as an opportunity to become more visible and memorable instead of something to avoid.

Good Public Speaking Skills Will Impact Your Career and Income

Good public speaking builds confidence, leadership skills and respect from management and your peers. When you prepare a presentation you become the subject expert which increases your knowledge.

In management and leadership roles you will need to be confident and comfortable speaking to others to get promoted. Questions to Consider:

1. Are you a member of a public speaking organization? Circle One

    Yes   or   No

2. Do you agree public speaking is essential for your career success? Circle One

    Yes   or   No

3. How would you rate your public speaking skills today? Circle One

    1. Excellent

    2. Very Good

    3. Good

    4. Average

    5. Improvement Needed

4. Have you avoided public speaking for fear you might make a mistake and be embarrassed? Circle One

    Yes   or   No

5. Do your public speaking skills need improvement? Circle One

Yes or No

Based on your responses to these questions you may have room for improvement. Use the following plan to get started.

Public Speaking Skills Plan

1. Join a public speaking organization. Ask your human resources department about local chapters.

2. Practice making presentions in small groups to build your confidence.

3. Ask for feedback from someone you trust and respect.

4. Strengthen the areas of concern.

5. Volunteer to make presentations in small groups to increase your self-confidence and career opportunities.

6. If you have excellent or very good public speaking skills – are you using your skills to advance your career and increase your income? Circle one

Yes or No

If no – what is your plan to gain more exposure for public speaking?

1. _____

2. _____

3. _____

7. What action steps are you willing to take immediately to improve public speaking skills?

Action Steps:

1. _____

2. _____

3. _____

4. _____

5. _____

Public speaking skills will open doors – poor skills will close them. The key to being good at public speaking is – research your topic, prepare your presentation and practice out loud several times before you present to an audience. Practice builds your confidence. You may choose to present to a peer or your manager before you present to others.

Pay close attention how you speak – do not speak too fast it shows you are nervous and increases your chances of errors. Pause between topics and do not read every word in your presentation or from note cards.

Do you prefer to speak behind a podium or interact with your audience? A podium creates a barrier between you and your audience which allows you to feel safe. Instead of speaking behind a podium interact with your audience. Your movement, voice and appropriate hand gestures make your presentation interactive, passionate and memorable. To become an exceptional public speaker use the following tips to guide you.

1. Research your topic.

2. Plan and organize your presentation.

3. Be the subject expert.

4. Practice your presentation out loud so you can hear how you sound.

5. Avoid presenting your entire presentation behind a podium – interact with your audience.

6. Be aware of your body language.

7. Overcome fear with confidence.

Public speaking raises the awareness of your skills by your manager and other executives who may attend your presentation. There is no doubt you will need to speak in a group environment as part of your role at work. While you may be fearful the benefits of having public speaking skills in your career portfolio out weigh the perceived fears.

Be Happy At Work Essentials

1. Good public speaking skills impact your career and income.

2. Public speaking skills are a requirement in the workplace.

3. Public speaking builds leadership skills.

4. Overcome public speaking fears with self-confidence.

Chapter 18

How to Be Accountable for Your Happiness at Work

Employees often believe their employer is responsible for their happiness at work. The reality is you are responsible for your happiness at work. All employees have career options – it's up to each person to take the initiative to improve your current status to be happier at work. Use these happiness rules to be accountable.

Twenty One Happiness Rules

Rule 1: Accountable. Be accountable for work assigned to you.

Rule 2: Attitude. Your attitude impacts your relationships and career success.

Rule 3: Be Positive. Avoid negative conversations, gossip and unhappy people.

Rule 4: Body Language. Be aware of your non-verbal body language.

Rule 5: Celebrate Progress. Celebrate progress you make to achieve goals.

Rule 6: Commitments. Make only commitments you can keep.

Rule 7: Do Something You Love. Do something you love everyday outside of work.

Rule 8: Enthusiasm. Show enthusiasm in everything you do.

Rule 9: Eye Contact. Establish good eye contact with everyone.

Rule 10: Feedback. Ask your manager for feedback about your performance.

Rule 11: Good Night Sleep. Get a good night sleep every night.

Rule 12: Happiness at Work. Be accountable for your happiness at work.

Rule 13: Job Search. When all else fails re-evaluate your employer, job and career.

Rule 14: Make Friends at Work. Friends provide caring, resources, sharing and support.

Rule 15: Make Great Decisions. Know when to say "no" to tasks which are non-urgent and not a priority.

Rule 16: Meaningful Conflict. Practice meaningful conflict to accomplish company goals.

Rule 17: Professional Development. Take ownership of your professional development.

Rule 18: Public Speaking. Good public speaking skills increases career options.

Rule 19: Responsibility. Take responsibility for your job description.

Rule 20: Self-Confidence. Self-confidence opens doors to new career opportunities.

Rule 21: Walk Away from Toxic People. Spend time with happy people.

Chapter 19

The Career Benefits of Joining a Professional Association

Are you a member of a Professional Association? A professional association increases your knowledge; jump starts your job search and builds your network with industry professionals. Almost all industries have professional associations which provide valuable resources for career advancement. Many associations have national, state and regional chapters which you can join. Discover how a professional association membership can benefit your career.

Eight Ways a Professional Association Can Benefit Your Career

1. *Code of Ethics.* It's important to know and understand the code of ethics and what is considered best practice in your industry.

2. *Conferences.* Members can attend industry conferences, conventions and workshops at a discount rate to see keynote speakers.

During your job search you can impress an employer by knowing the trends, issues, changes and progress in your industry.

You can find out what other organizations are doing, meet the speakers and other professionals to build your network.

3. *Employment.* Professional associations list internships and employment opportunities on their websites which may not be advertised on job boards. Membership shows you are involved and committed to your industry.

4. *Industry Standards.* Membership provides continuing education, certification programs, webinars and e-newsletters to keep you informed about industry standards.

5. *Knowledge.* Membership offers a wealth of information about internships, employment, industry issues and trends which can affect your career plans. You can be connected with key speakers, decision makers and knowledge of new developments.

Membership provides access to career-related topics, journals, articles, books, white papers, newsletters, magazines, scholarship information and links to industry publications.

A job seeker who references a speaker, trend, certification or other association information during an interview will show you are knowledgeable about your industry.

6. *Networking.* Networking with other professionals allows you to ask for advice, build trust, help others achieve their goals, share ideas, get support and volunteer to be on a committee or a guest speaker.

   Volunteering in a leadership role is a great way to learn from others and enhance your professional development.

   Networking allows you to find a mentor or mentor someone else. Giving back to others can be the greatest reward.

7. *Research.* The best way to determine which association is best for you is to visit their websites, ask for recommendations from management and your peers. Find out about benefits and requirements for memberships. You may choose to be an associate member through your company or an individual membership which may cost more than an associate membership.

8. *Updates and Policies.* Membership provides legislation updates on policies which may affect changes in your industry.

Membership Advantage

Professional association membership is an excellent investment for your future. Membership promotes career advancement, builds your industry network, professional development and career options for you to explore.

Be Happy at Work Essentials

1. A professional association membership will help advance your career.

2. Know the code of ethics for your industry.

3. Conferences are a great place to hear and meet keynote speakers in your field.

4. Membership provides internships and employment opportunities not advertised on job boards.

5. Membership shows you are involved and committed to your industry.

6. Membership provides a wealth of information which pertains to your industry.

7. Membership provides access to career related topics and resources.

8. Membership allows you to build your network with industry professionals.

BE HAPPY AT WORK

Build strong and internal and external relationships to expand your network.

Enthusiasm is the energy which brings about successful results.

Happiness comes from within.

A happy you at work begin with personal accountability.

Plan for career success.

Personal branding is a career distinction which differentiates you from others.

You are accountable for your happiness at work.

Ask for career advice from sponsors, mentors, managers and career coaches.

Trust is the foundation for meaningful relationships for career growth.

Write your career vision, mission and goals and take action.

Opportunities do not necessarily come to you – you have to make it happen.

Risk empowers you to expand your thinking and set new boundaries.

Knowledge and wisdom are essential keys to success.

CONCLUSION

Happiness A Personal Responsibility

Be Happy: How To Be Happy At Work and Be A Happier You - provides new strategies you can implement to improve your outlook at work and happiness today. Everyday you have a choice to be happy at work. Those who are happy are more enthusiastic, motivated, energized and productive than their unhappy peers. No matter what your generation, current position or title you are accountable for your own happiness.

Happiness at work does not tend to go hand in hand – it's estimated less than 15% of people consider themselves happily engaged at work. Take control of your happiness and identify why you are unhappy. Are you in a dead end job? Do you lack the motivation to do the same thing every day? Are there no opportunities for advancement? Are you being skipped over for promotion? Do you dislike your company, boss, culture and people you work with? Are you doing everything in your power to be happy at work? Once you identify why you are unhappy – make a career plan to recharge your happiness and love your work and environment.

Build successful relationships to accomplish work goals, get salary increases and promotions. Be a good listener, support your coworkers and be nice to everyone. Reach out to new colleagues and get to know a little about each one on your team. Learn about their backgrounds, successes, interests, volunteer work and something unrelated to work to get to know them. Positive work relationships allow you to accomplish work goals and be happy.

A sponsor will help you develop a strategic career plan to fast track your career and build senior relationships. Sponsors provide career advice, guidance, help develop you as a leader, provide career support so you can take smart calculated risks.

Personal branding is your career distinction to stand out in any economy and industry. Build your visibility by creating your personal brand within your organization. Sell your brand for internal promotions and external new career opportunities. Look for ways to interact with top management at meetings and conferences. Volunteer for projects and committees to meet executives and other peers. Use your personal and intellectual assets to differentiate you from others.

Employers are attracted to candidates who invest their time in continuous learning – the college degree you have is no longer enough. Boost your career by taking an online course, getting a certificate, teaching a class at a university, obtain a degree, get an advanced degree or participate in professional development courses offered by your employer. The candidate who gets hired or promoted the fastest are those who invest in their careers.

"You have the power to be happy at work"
-Patricia Dorch

ABOUT THE AUTHOR

PATRICIA DORCH, a Senior Consultant for Right Management. Right Management is a provider of Career Transition and Job Search Coaching to professionals in transition. Right Management is the global career and talent development expert within ManpowerGroup (NYSE:MAN). She has a Master of Science in Business Organizational Management from the University of La Verne – La Verne, CA, Bachelor of Fine Arts from Pratt Institute – Brooklyn, NY. Patricia's background includes Career Coach, Career Transition, Career Management, Workforce Development, Training and Development and Sales and Marketing.

Patricia is the author of *What Are Soft Skills? How To Master Essential Skills To Achieve Workplace Success, Professionalism: New Rules for Workplace Career Success, Job Search: College Graduates New Career Advice, Ideas and Strategies to Get Hired, Military To Civilian Transition: Job Search Strategies and Tips to Get Hired in the Civilian Job Market, Job Search: New Get Hired Ideas, Tips and Strategies for 40 Plus, Six Figure Career Coaching Advice: The Ultimate Guide to Achieving Success, Job Search: Teen Interview Tips and Strategies to Get Hired and Be Happy: How To Be Happy At Work and Be A Happier You.*

Available At:

www.amazon.com and barnesandnoble.com

Are you looking for a dynamic speaker? Patricia's enthusiasm and passion is what you want for your next training or special event. Her energy is contagious and will have your audience on their feet with excitement. Schedule her for your next conference, meeting, educational program, regional or local training.

Book Review:

You are invited to write a book review at: www.amazon.com and www.barnesandnoble.com Thank you for sharing your positive feedback.

Website: www.howtobehappyatworkbook.com
Email: Patricia@howtobehappyatworkbook.com

Website: www.whataresoftskills.net
Email: Patricia@whataresoftskills.net

Website: www.whatisprofessionalism.com
Email: Patricia@whatisprofessinalism.com

Website:
www.jobsearchcollegegraduatesbook.com

Email:
Patricia@jobsearchcollegegraduatesbook.com

Website: www.militarytociviliantransition.net
Email: Patricia@militarytociviliantransition.net

Conferences, Educational Programs, Events, Meetings, Retreats, Town hall Meetings and Training and Development

Are you a Top Executive, Manager, Executive Assistant, Meeting Planner, Program Manager, Purchasing Manager, Training Manager or someone who is in charge of which giveaways should be included in your business event? If so, *Be Happy* is the ultimate educational gift to give to your employees.

Be Happy: How To Be Happy At Work and Be A Happier You - effective techniques, tools and new strategies will get employees motivated, excited and enthusiastic about being happy at work every day. Employees will learn the importance and benefits of "continuous learning" and how new skills build confidence and empower them to be marketable for career opportunities. Happy employees improve retention, reduce hiring cost and increase productivity – that's something to be happy about!

Make your employees happy – give them *Be Happy*.

Order Books:
www.amazon.com
www.barnesandnoble.com

Professional Resources

Business and Job Search Books

PROFESSIONAL·ISM

Professionalism
New Rules
for Workplace
Career Success

PATRICIA DORCH

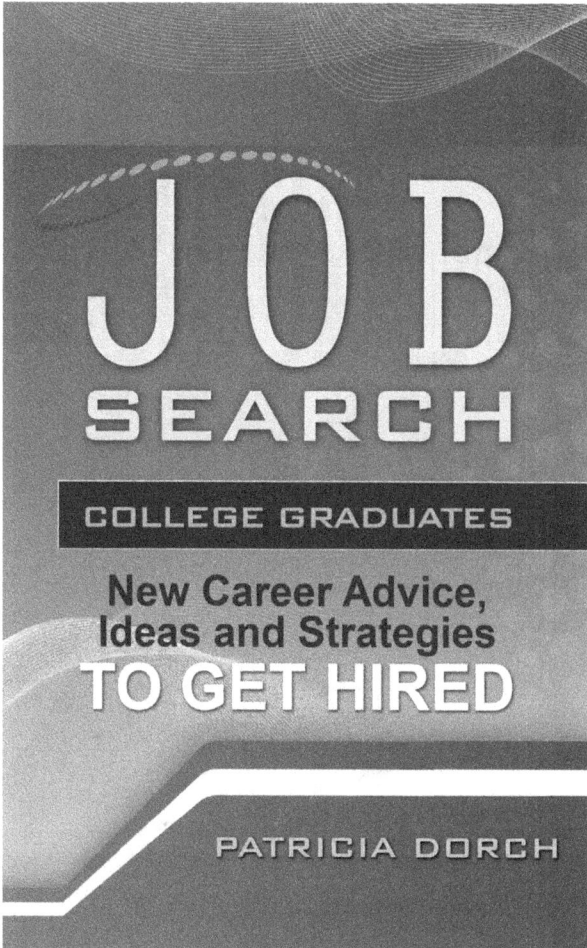

JOB
SEARCH

COLLEGE GRADUATES

New Career Advice,
Ideas and Strategies
TO GET HIRED

PATRICIA DORCH

MILITARY TO CIVILIAN TRANSITION JOB Search Strategies and Tips to GET HIRED in the CIVILIAN JOB MARKET

PATRICIA DORCH

JOB SEARCH

TEEN
INTERVIEW TIPS AND STRATEGIES TO
GET HIRED

PATRICIA DORCH

SIX FIGURE
CAREER
COACHING
ADVICE

PATRICIA DORCH

THE ULTIMATE GUIDE
TO ACHIEVING SUCCESS

Job Search

New
Get Hired
Ideas, Tips and
Strategies for
40 Plus

PATRICIA DORCH

BE HAPPY

How To Be Happy At Work and Be A Happier You

PATRICIA DORCH

Job Search

New
Get Hired
Ideas, Tips and
Strategies for
40 Plus

PATRICIA DORCH

BE HAPPY

How To Be Happy At Work and Be A Happier You

PATRICIA DORCH

www.ingramcontent.com/pod-product-compliance
Lightning Source LLC
Chambersburg PA
CBHW060031210326
41520CB00009B/1088